Let's Go Visit

Best Friends
Animal Sanctuary

An Educational Children's Adventure Teaching Responsible Pet
Ownership and Animal Rescue Ideals to Kids!

by

Nola Lee Kelsey

DogsEyeViewPress
P.O. Box 888
Hot Springs, SD USA 57747

ISBN: 978-0-9802323-0-1

Library of Congress Control Number: 2007910118

Printed in the United States of America.

Cover design by Nola L. Kelsey
Edited by Jeanne Modesitt

All photographs are by Nola L. Kelsey except where otherwise credited.

Front cover photographs

Luna the miniature horse, Sean the goat, Elias F. with Ella the conure, Theresa the dog, Scooter the cat at the Best in Show contest, and the Scheurich family takes a "pig tour".

Back cover photographs

Jiggle cat, Zena (photograph by Jose Pico) Bunny Blue, and Gypsy.

Dedicated with all my heart to Tex and all

The Lodge Dogs of Best Friends,

each one a treasured Angel in Waiting for the heavenly gift of
a loving and forever, one-dog family!

Tex

Meet them all at:
http://network.bestfriends.org/lodgedogs/news

Welcome to Best Friends

Visiting an ice cream parlor might tickle your tongue.

Visiting an amusement park could tickle your tummy.

Visiting Best Friends Animal Sanctuary will tickle your heart. It's true! And, after reading this book, you'll understand why. Let's go visit Best Friends now.

First of all, do you know what an animal sanctuary is? An animal sanctuary is a safe place for animals to live. Best Friends Animal Sanctuary is the largest sanctuary in the United States for abused and abandoned pets. There are usually about 1,500 animals living at Best Friends. Imagine having that many pets.

With so many critters around, you may wonder, don't they run out of places to keep them? Are they stacking up the puppies like pyramids or letting the birds swing from the chandeliers? No. Best Friends is just big! Really big!

In fact, Best Friends has over thirty three thousand acres of land in Southern Utah. How much land is that? Well, most people's yards at home are much less than one half of an acre. Try closing your eyes tight and imagining 100,000 backyards all stuck together. That's a lot of room to keep animals on, don't you think?

Winston

Frodo

Alan K. Anderson

So, what kinds of animals are at Best Friends? Why are they there? And, how do people help them? Follow along. You'll learn what you can see and do when visiting Best Friends. You can even meet some of the animals and find out where they came from. Their stories will teach you what Best Friends is all about. Oh, by the way, you can open your eyes now.

You will definitely open your eyes wide when you enter Angel Canyon.

This is the canyon where the sanctuary is located. Towering red cliffs stand along the canyon road. Near the entrance caves can be seen high up along these cliffs. It's fun to imagine yourself exploring inside them. But there is more to Angel Canyon than just cliffs and caves.

Ancient Indian archeological sites, Hollywood film locations, a winding creek, and hiking trails all tell arriving visitors they are in for a unique adventure. With so much to see you might wonder where your visit to Best Friends should start. Here's an idea, how

Cupid helps out in the gift shop

about starting at the Welcome Center?

Free tours of the sanctuary leave the Welcome Center throughout the day. Visitors can also watch a film about Best Friends or spend their parent's hard-earned money in the gift shop. The shop is packed with souvenirs and presents, each with an animal theme. There are even treats and toys for your pets back home. After all, animals are the point of visiting Best Friends. But where are all the sanctuary animals?

A barn originally built for the movie set of One Little Indian

Above: Luna the mini shows off her prize

Below: A playful goat named Sean

Horse Haven

The animals are everywhere! One of the first things you'll see as you approach the Welcome Center is an area called Horse Haven. Would you like to guess why it's called Horse Haven? If you guessed that Horse Haven is where the parrots live, ask someone to see if you have a fever. Oddly enough, Horse Haven is where Best Friends keeps many of their horses. Are you really that surprised?

There are barns, corrals, stalls, offices, and lots of big pastures at Horse Haven. Keep an eye out for Cowboy, the swaybacked quarter-horse. The people who take care of horses at Best Friends say Cowboy acts like a 1,000 pound dog. He loves to just hang around people and play like a puppy. An extremely big puppy!

For some people, a playful horse is not a good enough horse. Cowboy's first owners wanted a working horse that was built to ride. That was not a great job for a guy with a swayback. They were thinking of having Cowboy killed, just because he could not do the type of work they wanted him to do. Now he works bringing smiles to the faces of Best Friends' visitors. That's the best job of all for Cowboy, wouldn't you agree?

Other fun farm animals live at Horse Haven as well. Sebaastian and Baa Baa Ganoush, two woolly sheep, graze quietly in the fields while playful goats like Thelma and Louise race and chase around rock piles. Crazy goat antics are fabulously silly to watch. Still, Horse Haven's goofiest residents may be its pigs. Just listen to their oinks and grunts as they waddle past you quickly on absurdly, stubby little legs.

Swayback Cowboy

Potbellies named Raisin, Brittany, Cherry, Jack, and Jake all pass their days peacefully in extra fancy pig sties. While you probably shouldn't keep your own room like a pig sty, it's just the way it should be for these sweet swine. They are right at home.

Two of these pigs, Jeffery and Hogan, were rescued from an animal hoarder. Hoarders are people who keep lots of animals. In fact, they have more animals than they have time or money to properly care for. Hoarders often think they are rescuers. They are not!

Jeffery and Hogan lived on less than one small acre with 250 other pigs. Yuck! That's not a recipe for a happy life. Cats, chickens, ducks, and other animals lived there too. The hoarder had around 500 animals total in this little bitty space. Double yuck! This was a big, pig mess!

Every time these poor fellows moved, they bumped into another animal. The awful hoarders never had time to pay attention to so many critters, so Jeffrey and Hogan grew up shy. They were not used to people at all. Both of these pigs were easily scared by lots of things. Plus, they never got the piggy perfect health care they needed.

Pig Caregiver Yvonne treats Jeffery and Hogan to an in-between meal snack.

Sebaastian peeks at visitors.

Daphne models her new faux leather jacket.

Caregiver Linda demonstrates Parelli Natural Horsemanship training with the help of Faith the horse.

Finally, the town where the hoarders lived stepped in. "You can't do that," they said. "It's wrong!" The town contacted a shelter in California for help. Then Best Friends offered to lend a hand and take care of some of the rescued animals.

Good news! Jeffery and Hogan now live at the sanctuary. They have veterinarians (animal doctors), caregivers, and visitors all looking out for them. They even have a comfortable, roomy new sty where they can stretch out for a nap in the sun or waddle around all day long. Things are looking much better for this fabulous piggy pair. Make sure you ask about a 'pig tour' when you visit Best Friends. The boys would love to say, hello.

When you leave Horse Haven and drive further into Angel Canyon, you'll see more livestock pastures. Best Friends has lots of room on which to keep other rescued horses, donkeys, and burrows. Watch for old Grandpa Bernie the singing burro and his new girlfriend Grandma Willow. These big eared seniors are Best Friends hottest new old couple.

Veterinary Technician Aubrey gently works with Buster Brown

Bunny House

As you wind up the cliff to Angel Canyon's rim, be prepared. It's not far now to The Land of Wiggles and Giggles. You're about to enter the Bunny House. In fact, in 2007, Best Friends built a new bigger, better, bunny building. It's beautiful! You might even call it bunnyreffic. One thing's for sure, this place has more wiggling noses per square foot than any other place at Best Friend's. That makes it easy for Bunny House visitors to turn into gigglers.

Rose and Clay cuddle in the sunshine.

Bunny Blue waits to be adopted by a forever-family.

Two rabbits loose together can quickly become many rabbits if they are not fixed.

Photograph by Alan K. Anderson

Most of the rescued rabbits at Bunny House are simply going about their happy bunny days while they wait for a special family to come and adopt them. They've each had their special bunny shots and have all been spayed or neutered. That means the veterinarians have 'fixed' them so they are not able to have baby bunnies. Why? This is very important with pets, especially rabbits! Bunnies that have not been 'fixed' can have lots and lots of babies. Really lots! In fact, so many pet bunnies are born each year that there are never enough homes for them all. That's why Best Friends gives rabbits a great place to live at the sanctuary. Even if some are not adopted by families, they will have happy, hoppy lives right here. Only a forever family could be better.

One beautiful Best Friends bunny named Ellie, and several of the other rabbits at Bunny House, came to Best Friends from Reno, Nevada. A well-meaning, bunny-loving lady started out with just a few rabbits as pets. She did not know they could be fixed. Surprise! She quickly learned that bunnies are faster at multiplication than most math teachers. Within a few years, she had over a thousand rascally rabbits romping rambunctiously all around her yard. Oh my! The woman called Best Friends for help. She realized one person could not take care of them all. Her pets had become a big, bouncing problem!

Caregiver Danette with Athena

Max gets ready for the Best in Show contest

Feathered Friends

Not far up the road from Bunny House is Feathered Friends. This is where Mother Nature shows off her prettiest colors. Parrots, ducks, pigeons, peacocks, and more entertain visitors just by being fabulously beautiful to look at and fluttering around. Even the bird caregivers seem to fly about the area. They bring the birds fresh food, take animals outside to sun, clean the cages, fill up water dishes, and answer questions from visitors.

Don't miss the Parrot Garden. When you enter the garden, chatty Parrots say, "Hello" and may even give you a playful whistle. This gorgeous area is peaceful with plenty of shady benches to relax on while you hide from the desert sun. Trickling sounds from a waterfall sing in the background. In the distance Echo, a red tailed hawk, spies on you through the juniper trees. You can even take photos of many different kinds of parrots from chirpy little cockatiels to colorful giant macaws.

One parrot, a Moluccan Cockatoo named Seppi, is rumored to be a writer for Best Friends Magazine. His column is called Squawk Box. True, no one has actually seen Seppi do anything more than bite a computer during the daytime; still his caregivers believe he must write at night. That's when Feathered Friends is quietest. It's said that Seppi always manages to email his work to the editor on time. He's a big show off!

Ruby shows off her new tail growth

Rio grows healthier every day

Seppi takes a break from writing.

Elias and Ella enjoy the sun.

Frodo takes a nap.

For some of the birds at Feathered Friends, this is their second sanctuary home. What? How can that happen? Here's one way. Samantha, a green-winged Macaw, and seventeen of her feathered pals came to Best Friends after the small shelter they lived at ran out of enough money to take care of them. Sadly, it had to close. Luckily for the birds, they came to Best Friends. Here they will live happily ever after.

Many parrots live to be over sixty years old. Often they outlive their owners and sometimes they even outlive their shelters. It's a good thing Best Friends is such a large operation. There are lots of people of all ages caring for the animals. Plus, many other generous people make donations to help pay the cost of caring for the animals. Because Best Friends is so big and well-known, they will be here to offer homes to homeless pets for many years to come – even long living parrots.

Merlynne and Indigo

If webbed feet give you a laugh, Cedar the duck is waiting to meet you. She is definitely one plucky ducky. A while back Cedar and her boyfriend were attacked by a dog. Her boyfriend died and she was hurt quite badly. But time really does heal many wounds!

This spunky water fowl would not let a few permanent injuries or bad past experiences get her down. She chose to live life to the fullest. Not only is Cedar a whole new duck, she is also a bit of a social butterfly. She's grown healthy and strong, made new friends, and has charmed the guy ducks right out of their pools. After all, what's a little scar tissue where true love is concerned? It's what's in a duck's heart that matters. And that is the quackin' big truth!

Sidney

Milton

Cat World

Up the road from Feathered Friends is Cat World. Here Best Friends gives shelter to every manner of fantastic feline friend. There are old cats, young cats, fat cats and small cats. Some arrived sick or injured. Some came here as kittens. But all dream of the joy of finding a life-long home. One thing is for sure: the cats of Cat World have some very snazzy living quarters. Just wait until you check out the catteries. Wowza!

Catteries are specialized cat homes. Look around one and think about the design. Each cattery has indoor and outdoor rooms with several cat doors in-between. There are cubby holes to hide in and tall poles to climb. Good catteries have oodles of places to scratch, to play, to hide, and to nap. Cats can even tiptoe through the rafters of the ceiling to find a place to spy on you or slip under a box on the floor to use the litter tray. Privacy please! Everything is designed with the deluxe kitty lifestyle in mind. Wouldn't it be cool to have a super-sized cattery for people to play in?

When visiting Cat World, keep an eye out for Abby. But beware. If you dare to enter someone else's cattery, she won't be very happy with you. This charismatic, clinging kitty wants all the love she can sink her paws into. She'll even scale the walls of her room just so you'll notice her. Abby is a bit like a spider monkey that purrs.

Abby gets ready to pounce

Each of the cats in Cat World is unique. So are the reasons they have come to live at Best Friends. Take Oliver (a.k.a. Oliver the Bad Man), for example. He snuggles and loves you one second, then bounces off the walls the next. No one knows why. But at Best Friends, Oliver is allowed to be himself. He is the very best Oliver around. That's what makes him special. Can you imagine how dull it would be if every cat everywhere looked and acted exactly the same all the time? Ho hum.

Opie

Another kitty, Opie, used to be a stray. He was found trapped inside a storm drain. While on his daily walks, a dog kept telling his owner, "Ah, hey, there's something down there." After a couple days the dog's owner looked to see what all the fuss was about. It's a good thing the owner finally listened! Opie had nearly starved to death. Veterinarians discovered that not only had the hungry kitty been hit by a car, he also had a disease called diabetes. Ugh! When you're a stray, needing daily medicine can be a real problem!

As a result of all his bad luck, Opie's back legs don't work very well. But, good luck finally won over. Thanks to care and attention from the Best Friends staff this disabled kitty was given a second chance at life. You can see how happy he is. Sure, Opie walks a bit different. So what! You just can't keep a good kitty down.

One of the favorite jobs for volunteers visiting Best Friends is to 'socialize' cats. Socializing means getting them used to being around people. When an animal is comfortable with people, they become more adoptable. Most folks want to adopt animals that are friendly and enjoy hanging out with them. It's just the way it is.

Could you socialize an animal? To socialize cats, people need to spend time with them. Some folks pet and groom the more relaxed kitties. Others sit inside the catteries and read books or play musical instruments. They patiently wait for the shy cats to come to them. Gosh, isn't that a tuff job?

Lovebug

Oliver

Lucinda

Pokey

Martha celebrates getting a new toy!

Dogtown

Once you have had your fill of fur balls and purr balls, it's time to visit Dogtown. Say goodbye to peace and quiet! This is where Best Friends' wildest bunch of misfits steals hearts. Before coming to the sanctuary, many of the Dogtown residents lived with hoarders or in dreadful places called puppy mills. Others were abused, neglected, abandoned or lived their lives chained up. No one cared or even thought about the dog's feelings. That's never fun for anyone.

Happily, when you visit Dogtown you are visiting The Land of Second Chances. Rescued dogs wait for new families to adopt them. A life-long home full of the love is what every canine deserves. And, just like with cats, having visitors stop by makes the dogs' lives even better. Your love and attention is the greatest gift you can give them while on your visit.

Martha

Most of the dogs in Dogtown live in Octagons. These are eight sided buildings. Look inside. On most sides of the octagons you will see large indoor doggie bedrooms which are heated in winter and cooled in the summer. What a 'ruff' life! The bedrooms have doors that lead out to big fenced yards called runs. Groups of two or more dogs live in each run. They have toys, shade trees, swimming pools, dog houses, and more toys. Can dogs ever have enough toys? No way!

One of the best parts about meeting the dogs of Dogtown is learning their stories. Just ask a caregiver. Every dog has its own special story. Take Animal, for example. Animal came to Best Friends from Nebraska where he had spent his entire life in a puppy mill.

Apple was rescued from a puppy mill.

Puppy mills are places that exist only to breed puppies to sell for money. The pups' parents often live their whole lives in small dingy cages. Many don't ever get to run or even play, and they never know the joy of having their own family. These adult dogs are just used as puppy making machines.

Animal

It's hard for the puppies, too. They may be taken from their parents when they are too young, and then sold to pet stores only to be sold again to someone else. If the puppies are not perfect, they might even be killed. Puppy mills are very bad businesses!

Since Animal grew up in a puppy mill, he never learned to love and play, just fight and bite. Fortunately for Animal and his friends, the mill they lived at was closed down. Nebraska Humane Society began rescuing the dogs and staff from Best Friends flew to Omaha, Nebraska to help with some of the animals.

Now, dog trainers and caregivers at Best Friends Sanctuary are slowly teaching Animal that he is safe and loved. He'll never live isolated in a cramped little cage again. He doesn't need to bite people and chase them away. Soon Animal will understand there are good people in the world he can trust. That will be a big step toward finding him a family of his very own.

Once you visit Best Friends, you will understand why pet stores should just sell pet supplies – not living animals. Most customers at pet stores do not know puppies come from such terrible places. If they did, they would never shop for living animals at a store. It wouldn't be right! Pets are loving, feeling beings, not merchandise!

Dog Trainer Whitney helps Animal adjust to being handled.

Wouldn't it be great for all dogs like Animal if every puppy mill closed down? Imagine if families adopted all their pets from sanctuaries and shelters instead of buying them in shops. Think about it. Pet stores would not stock what they could not sell. Puppy mills would have to close down if they did not have pet stores as paying customers. Rescued dogs living in shelters could find homes with the families that were caring enough not to shop for animals in stores. Soon there could be no more homeless pets.

Wow! People's choices do make a big difference in the lives of animals. You can be an example to others and your own actions can help change the world. These are some of the best lessons you will learn from visiting Best Friends. But, why wait? Next time your family wants to adopt a pet for life, tell them you would like to save a shelter animal. They'll be proud!

Visitors often notice that dogs at Best Friends wear different colors of collars. Most are green or red. Just like a traffic light, green means go. If visitors get a caregiver's permission, they can go ahead and spend time with a green-collar dog. Lots of green-collar dogs live at Best Friends.

Also, like on a traffic light, red means stop. Red-collar dogs sometimes bite strangers and can not be handled by people they don't know. Having a red-collar does not mean a dog is bad. It only means that the dog may make a bad mistake and bite. Everyone can make mistakes. There are many reasons a dog might bite. Let's look at one dog's story.

During the summer of 2005, a hurricane called Katrina hit the city of New Orleans, Louisiana. The hurricane separated thousands of animals from their homes and families. One of those lost dogs was a big, goofy, rottweiler named Meatball. He was caught in a flood caused by the storm and was alone and scared for days. The flood water was full of harmful chemicals and debris. By the time rescuers from Best Friends found Meatball, he needed lots of medical care. And, he did not like all those medical treatments given by the scary strangers one bit! Who would?

Above green-collar Valentine and below red-collar Twyla each enjoy toys in their own special way

Volunteer Gerry works with Rufus.

Nichole moves in for a kiss.

Ruben and Frogi relax in the shade.

Volunteer Kelly plays with Synergy.

Brandon proves even the biggest dogs can have a green collar.

Now Meatball is scared of strangers. He suspects they might be sneaky veterinary doctors, coming after him with shots and band aids, so he puts on a big tough guy act to chase them away. Do you know anyone who acts mean because they don't want you to see how scared they are? Sometimes people do that as well. Fortunately for Meatball, he loves cookies. Lots and lots of cookies!

Food is the key to the big guy's heart. It helps him to relax. Once he gets used to a special caregiver feeding him his favorite food (which is almost anything that's edible), Meatball allows them into his dog run – to give him more cookies, of course. After he is adjusts to the person being in his run, they are even permitted to play fetch with his favorite toys. In time, Meatball trusts his caregivers enough to allow them to walk him on a leash or take him to the Best Friends' dog park to play. Walks and playing relax him even more.

Meatball loves to bounce around the park chasing lizards. During the chase, bushes and small trees get launched in every direction. Don't worry though, he never comes close to catching a lizard, but he thinks he does. That's all that matters. Why? Because Meatball is not a tough guy, after all. He's just a big, silly clown!

Meatball

You know you're in good with Meatball when he lets you rub his tummy. And what a big tummy it is! Do you think when you grow up you might take the time to build a friendship with a scared animal or person? It can take a lot of patience. Still, imagine how special it is to finally be shown that big Meatball tummy for the very first time. That's a heart tickler worth a thousand ice cream cones!

Other animals at Best friends were also rescued from what are called catastrophic events. Catastrophic events are gigantic disasters. You'll meet more disaster survivors on your visit to the sanctuary. Martha, another Hurricane Katrina Dog, has a green collar and is a favorite of visitors who like to take dogs out on hikes or have an evening of cuddling in town. Martha loves kids!

Meatball is one of Best Friends biggest clowns.

Glouton

Vega plays with Dixie.

Champ

Flower

Slow, huggable Glouton; tall, lanky Champ; happy, playful Vega; and sweet, beautiful Flower are four of Best Friends' "Lebanon Dogs." Can you find Lebanon on a map? Hint, it's about 7,000 miles east of Utah.

Glouton, Champ, Vega, and Flower all traveled a long way when they were rescued from a war zone in that far off country. Best Friends moved almost 300 of these special animal refugees to the sanctuary in Angel Canyon. The journey took two whole days. They even flew across the Atlantic Ocean.

Shy Sly

Animals crossing oceans! Rescues in New Orleans! Rabbits from Reno! Puppy mill dogs saved in Nebraska! At the sanctuary you will even visit animals from Hawaii, New York, Alaska, and more. When visiting Best Friends it's always fun to bring along an atlas or globe. Then you can look and see where all the different critters came from.

Better still, people can do more than take a tour when visiting Best Friends. Why not socialize with the cats? Or, your family could volunteer to take a dog on drive to help it get used to riding in cars. Dogs can even go on hikes or on overnight visits to town with you. By having your parents ask to take a kid-friendly dog on an adventure, you help the pups stay socialized.

Socialization is as important for dogs, as it is for cats. Remember the more socialized an animal is, the better chance it has of being adopted by a forever family. Again, you have the power to make a difference. Think about this. An amusement park roller coaster may be a blast for 5 minutes, but playing with a dog can change its life forever. (And, there are no long lines to stand in.) Isn't that a cool way to make your visit to Best Friends extra special?

Caregivers Mileen & Megan say goodbye to an adopted Howard

Some of the favorite dogs for outings live at Old Friends. This area is Dogtown's senior citizen center. It's made up of two octagons, but there is no shuffleboard court here. Old Friends is where the older dogs live and get the special care they need. It's a popular place for tour stops and volunteers alike. Could you spend time with these mellow old hounds? Maybe you could even teach an old dog a new trick. Maybe not. But, it's always fun to try!

Kona, a favorite Old Friend

What other animals might be found at Best Friends? Can you guess? They scamper around everywhere. There are some at Horse Haven and the Bunny House. You can even find them at Feathered Friends, Cat World, and in Dogtown. What could they be? Did you guess? The final critters you can visit at Best Friends are the people!

Everywhere you go at the sanctuary, you'll see caregivers. These are people who are specialized in taking care of certain types of animals. There is a pig lady, bunny experts, bird men (and women), and wildlife keepers. Even cat people and dog people work side by side caring for the animals of Best Friends. Every caregiver enjoys teaching visitors about the animals they love. Ask them all your questions. But be careful. They might never stop talking.

Volunteers help Mr. Hope with a spinal problem by walking him often.

Volunteers also work at Best Friends. Volunteers are people who work for free. Can you imagine such a thing? Why would they work for free? Volunteers for the sanctuary love animals and want to help them. Some volunteers come for one day. Others spend their entire vacation at Best Friends. There are even volunteers who live nearby and help the animals all year long. It may be that volunteers have the most ticklish hearts of all.

Boomer was rescued from a hoarder in Hawaii.

Remember when you visit Best Friends, it takes more than just caregivers to run such a massive sanctuary. It is a business after all. Think about it. Close your eyes again. Imagine what types of people you would need to run any business this large. How many other types of sanctuary jobs can you think of? Count them on you fingers, nose, and toes.

Okay, go ahead and peek. How many jobs did you come up with? Did you count the tour guides that show visitors around or the cashiers in the gift shop? What about the writers and photographers for Best Friends Magazine? Seppi the parrot can't do it all himself.

There are also webmasters who run the website for Best Friends and technicians that keep the office computer systems working smoothly - most of the time. Did you think about the maintenance staff who keep the vehicles up and running, the floors clean and shiny, or that build all those dog runs?

In the medical clinic, there are veterinarians and vet nurses, assistants and techs. Best Friends has adoption specialists whose job it is to find the animals good homes. Trainers help animals, like Animal, with behavioral issues. In the dining hall, cooks keep the rest of the staff happy and well fed. Caregivers have big, big appetites!

Landscapers, teachers, secretaries, artists, fund raisers, and more all help keep this wonderful sanctuary up and running. Over 400 people work for Best Friends. Luckily each of them has his or her own special talent. Best Friends even has staff to find the best staff. They're called Human Resource Managers. And finally, Best Friends has volunteer coordinators. It's their job to work with the wonderful people who lend their hands for free.

What is your special talent? What type of work would you like to do? As you can see, all kinds of people are needed to work at Best Friends. Maybe someday you can too. Then you will be a part of helping animals live better lives and tickling the hearts of future visitors. What a terrific job that would be. Wouldn't you agree?

Vata tests out his new harness.

Hydrotherapist Carrie works with Kima.

Remington lounges behind his octagon while volunteers clean his dog run.

Rocky was chosen to go work with a Best Friends Training Partner.

Sweet Theresa shows off her favorite teddy bear to Adoption Specialist Kristi.

– Do and Learn –
How Can I Help Animals?

Buddha Speaks Up!
Write a play about rescuing an animal and perform it for your class or school.

As you have read there are lots of things you can do to help animals when you visit Best Friends. You can do even more at home. Want a project idea? The dogs from Best Friends have just the ticket for fun projects that individuals, groups, classrooms, or entire schools can do and learn from. Helping animals is as easy as picking your project and following it through to the end.

Dahlila Says Just Ask!
Call your local shelter and ask if they have any special projects you can help with.

Obed Treasures Art!
Draw posters reminding people to adopt shelter animals. Get permission hang them on local bulletin boards.

Astronomy Loves a Sale!
Have your classmates bring in items for a yard sale. Donate the money you raise to a local shelter.

Wildflower Likes Baby Steps
Ask your school to sponsor a shelter animal. Students can bring in all their family's pennies once a month to pay the sponsorship

Rex Writes!
Write a Letter to the Editor of your local newspaper. Tell readers about responsible pet ownership and kindness to animals.

Annie Helps Seniors!
Many Meals on Wheels programs deliver food for the pets of senior citizens. Have a pet food drive and donate what you collect.

Deja Watches Friends
If someone wants to adopt an animal just because they think it's cool remind them pets are many years of daily responsibility.

What is Sophie's Choice?
Hold a school car wash party and give the money you raise to help fund a low cost spayed/neuter program.

Do you have another great idea for how kids can help animals? We'd love to hear it.

Send us your ideas or photos and stories about what you have done to help animals.

Email: Let'sGoVisit@DogsEyeViewPress.com

Meatball Dreams Big!
Bring me cookies!

Mars

Most of the animals featured in this book were available for adoption from Best Friends Animal Society at the time of its publishing. If you would like to inquire about adoptions, view other animals available to loving homes, or learn more about Best Friends Animal Society visit their website at: www.BestFriends.org

For more ways to educate kids about animals contact the Best Friends Humane Education office at: Humane.ed@BestFriends.org

Photograph by Alan K. Anderson

More of Alan Anderson's photography can be seen at:
http://www.reflectedsun.com

Watch for more Let's Go Visit books at:
www.DogsEyeViewPress.com

Coming in September 2008,
Dogs: Funny Side Up! by Nola Lee Kelsey's

Ten percent of the profits from the sale of this book will be donated to animal rescue charities.